FOREST CLUB
FALL

A SEASON OF ACTIVITIES, CRAFTS, AND EXPLORING NATURE

KRIS HIRSCHMANN

ILLUSTRATED BY MARTA ANTELO

Quarto Library

Quarto is the authority on a wide range of topics.

Quarto educates, entertains and enriches the lives of our readers—enthusiasts and lovers of hands-on living.

www.quartoknows.com

Consultant: Anna Sharratt
Designer: Clare Barber
Editor: Emily Pither
Editorial Director: Laura Knowles
Art Director: Susi Martin
Creative Director: Malena Stojic
Group Publisher: Maxime Boucknooghe

This library edition published in 2020 by Quarto Library., an imprint of The Quarto Group.
26391 Crown Valley Parkway, Suite 220
Mission Viejo, CA 92691, USA
T: +1 949 380 7510
F: +1 949 380 7575
www.QuartoKnows.com

© 2021 Quarto Publishing plc

Distributed in the United States and Canada by Lerner Publisher Services
241 First Avenue North
Minneapolis, MN 55401 U.S.A.
www.lernerbooks.com

A CIP record for this book is available from the Library of Congress.

ISBN: 978-0-7112-6132-7

Manufactured in Guangdong, China CC092020
9 8 7 6 5 4 3 2 1

PICTURE CREDITS
Getty: 10tl Foodcollection.
Shutterstock: 6tl kelifamily, 6l AS Food studio, 6r Madlen, 6br TunedIn by Westend61, 10 grafvision, 10b osoznanie.jizni, 10r Dionisvera, 10cr YK, 12tl Nikolay Petkov, 12tc Madlen, 12tr rsooll, 12–13 ABTOP, Halina Valiushka, Lukasz Szwaj, maravan, 13 LilKar, 13r Platslee, 18tl vilax, 18l Richard Griffin, 18cl La corneja artesana, 18bl vilax, 18cb, 18tr AS Food studio, 18cr junyanjiang, 18br Richard Griffin.

Contents

Fruits of Fall

The forest bursts with bounty when autumn arrives. Plants hang heavy with fruits that started growing months earlier. Now they are finally full and ripe. What harvest-ready goodies might you find on a walk through the woods?

CAUTION! Some wild fruits are good to eat, but many are not. Some are even poisonous. **NEVER** eat anything you find without adult help and permission.

BERRIES
Blackberries and raspberries
Both of these berries have many juice-filled lobes. They grow on bushes and are good to eat, after washing.

Blackthorn berries
Blackthorn berries are deep blue and cloudy in color. Although they are edible, they can be bitingly bitter. Freeze and then thaw the berries to bring out their sweetness.

Rose hips
Rose hips are the fruits of the rose plant. They are delicious when made into jams and jellies. They can also be eaten raw, but watch out for the hairs inside. They'll tickle your tongue.

TREE FRUITS
Crabapples
Crabapple trees are usually small, with twisted trunks and gnarled limbs. They can be found throughout the world's forests. In the fall, they can be heavy with red, yellow, and orange fruit.

Plums
Wild plums are much smaller than the ones you buy in stores. They look a bit like grapes and are smooth, hairless, and round-oblong shaped. Not all plums are purple—they can also be red, yellow, or even green. If you pluck one from a tree and open it up, you'll find a rough, flat stone inside.

YEW

Danger! Poison!

Along with edible fruit, the fall forest is full of poisonous berries. Many of these berries are colorful and pretty to look at. Enjoy the spectacular colors and shapes of these fruits—but don't touch.

Yew

Bright orange yew berries have a large opening in one end. But watch out—the seed inside is deadly poisonous.

Holly

Holly berries add a splash of color wherever they grow. These solid little beauties are a treat for the eyes, but not the tongue.

POKEBERRY

HOLLY

Pokeberries

Pokeberries are easy to recognize by their vivid purple stems. These dark, shiny berries grow on low, spreading bushes with large green leaves.

NIGHTSHADE

Nightshade

Nightshade berries are glossy deep purple to black in color. They hang in clusters from tiny stems, looking like bunches of miniature eggplants.

ACTIVITY:
Berry Painting

Long before people could buy art supplies in stores, they used berry juice as paint. Try it yourself with materials you find in the forest.

This isn't just fun, it's a useful skill. You never know when you might need to write a message in the woods—or just when the creative urge might strike.

CAUTION! NEVER handle wild berries without expert adult help and permission.

YOU WILL NEED

- Berries (blueberries, blackberries, cherries, or raspberries, are good choices)
- Clear jar and spoon for each type of berry
- Water
- Plastic gloves
- Paintbrush
- White paper

How to do it

1 Put on plastic gloves to protect your hands. Carefully collect a small handful of berries, with adult supervision and help.

2 Put the berries into a jar. Add water until the berries are just covered.

3 Use a spoon to smash and stir the berries until the juice has mixed with the water.

4 Let the berries sit for a while, stirring occasionally. The longer you let them sit, the stronger the color will become.

5 Dip a paintbrush into the jar and use your berry paint to create a masterpiece on a piece of white paper.

Seeds

In the fall, many plants start to release seeds as they prepare for winter. Each seed contains everything it needs to grow into a new plant when the time and conditions are right. Seeds come in many shapes and sizes, and they spread in different ways. They find new places to rest for the winter and, hopefully, to survive until spring.

On the Air

Some seeds spread through the air. They drift on the wind, blowing here and there until they finally come to rest.

SEED HUNT

Look for seeds in the forest. How many different types can you find?

Floating Away

Some seeds drop into running water. They drift away on streams, rivers, lakes, and ocean currents. The water carries them to new places, where they may take root and grow. In this way, forests grow and expand.

Hitching a Ride

Some seeds are covered in tiny hooks. They attach themselves to animals' fur—or your clothes. They hitch a ride to a new place.

WALNUT

Nuts

Nuts are a type of seed. They tumble from trees and bushes in the fall. Like all seeds, a nut contains the information and materials it needs to grow into a new plant. If a nut ends up in a good growing area, it will rest all winter long—then sprout in the spring, when warmer weather arrives.

Walnuts are delicious. The soft, fleshy nut is protected by a tough case that is hard to crack open.

Acorns fall from oak trees. They are too bitter for most people, but many animals love them. The top of an acorn, called the cupule, looks a bit like a hat or a cap.

ACORN

CHESTNUT

BEECHNUT

Sweet chestnuts hide inside soft-spiked cases. People all over the world eat them as a tasty treat. Forest critters like them, too.

Beechnuts come from beech trees. Like sweet chestnuts, these nuts are protected by spiky cases.

Hazelnuts are round. They are protected by smooth, reddish-brown shells. The shells crack open by themselves when the nuts are ripe.

HAZELNUT

ANIMAL AID

Animals such as squirrels and birds help to spread nuts. They pluck nuts from plants or pick them up after they have fallen. They bury or hide the nuts to prepare for the long, hard winter ahead. They intend to come back and eat them later—but sometimes they forget. The buried nuts sit so long that they finally sprout into new plants.

ACTIVITY:
Nut Collecting

Although animals love nuts, they can't collect them all—trees make way too many! Next time you're out and about during fall, challenge a friend to a nut-collecting competition and see who can find the most. Can you spot any of the nuts shown on page 10? See how many different types of nut you can find!

Tips

1 Look on the floor for fresh, fallen nuts.

2 To work out the type of nut, try to identify the tree it came from.

3 Try using a magnifying glass to get a closer look.

ROWAN

RED OAK

BIRCH

Fall Leaves

In autumn, days get shorter and nights get longer. Trees sense the change in sunlight, and they start preparing for winter. A glorious process of color change begins.

Step 1: Turning Off

A tree starts "turning off" its leaves. It grows a special layer of cells to form a barrier between its leaves and branches.

Step 2: Green Gone

Leaves contain a green chemical called chlorophyll. When cold weather arrives, trees stop making new chlorophyll and green leaves start to fade.

ACER

BEECH

Step 3: Other Colors Emerge

The old chlorophyll breaks down and other colors, such as reds, yellows, oranges, and browns, become visible.

Step 4: Colors Brighten

The colors get brighter as the chlorophyll disappears and sunlight makes the colors even stronger.

Step 5: Leaves Fall

When the barrier between the branches and leaves is complete, the leaves can no longer cling to the tree. A light breeze or a shaking branch knocks them loose and they flutter to the ground.

ACTIVITY:
Leaf Wreath

Leaf wreaths bring a touch of fall color to your front door. Follow these easy instructions to build a wreath one leaf at a time as you move through the forest.

How to do it

1 Before you head outside, prepare your wreath base. Use scissors to cut a circle out of the center of the paper plate, leaving a doughnut shape. It should be about a finger length wide.

3 Continue adding leaves throughout your forest visit. Cover the entire doughnut.

4 When you return home, hang your leaf wreath on your front door.

2 Take your paper doughnut and look for pretty fallen leaves. When you find a leaf you like, use a glue stick to attach it to the doughnut. Dry leaves will stick best.

ACTIVITY:
Leaf Art

Make use of the autumn colors and natural materials to create your own piece of simple land art on the forest floor. Your artwork will naturally disappear, so no clearing up is required!

How to do it

1 Find an area on the floor and move any fallen objects aside to create a clear area to work on.

2 Use your imagination to visualize a pattern and place your natural materials on the ground to create your masterpiece. Experiment with materials, colors, and shapes.

3 Take a photograph of your art to capture it forever—the next time you visit, your artwork will have disappeared.

15

Breaking It Down

More and more leaves fall as autumn wears on and a brilliant blanket builds up, covering the forest floor. Underneath, minibeasts are swarming and material is rotting as everything decomposes, or breaks down.

Where to Look

Go Deep: Find an area where leaves are piled deep. Wearing gloves, gently push the layers of leaves aside. Use your senses—smell the rich humus and crinkle the dried leaves. As you dig deeper, you will find that the leaves are broken, smashed, and gooey. Which minibeasts can you see?

A HEALTHY FOREST

Decomposition is important to the forest's health. When leaves, sticks, and other plant matter break down, their nutrients are released. These chemicals enter the soil. They will rest there all winter long. In the spring, trees and other plants will suck up these nutrients through their roots. This natural fertilizer will help plants to make new leaves and branches. When autumn rolls around, the new material will fall and decompose, and the whole cycle will begin again.

Go Below: Thick fallen branches and logs trap moisture beneath them. Wearing gloves, gently lift these objects and peek under them for signs of rotting. How many types of minibeasts can you find?

Go Damp: Look in damp areas, such as pond edges, for signs of rotting. Can you spot any creepy crawlies?

MINIBEASTS

Many minibeasts aid decomposition by helping to break down fallen leaves and other organic material. These minibeasts are called decomposers.

Which minibeasts can you find?
- Spiders
- Beetles
- Millipedes
- Centipedes
- Slugs
- Snails
- Worms
- Woodlice
- Earwigs

BE CONSIDERATE

It is okay to move things to observe decomposition. When you are done looking, however, put everything back the way you found it. This is important to the health of the forest.

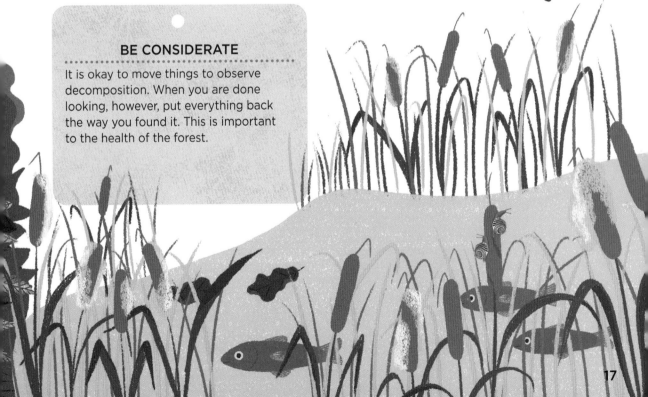

Fungi and Lichen

Fungi and lichen are not plants or animals. They are their own type of organism, or living thing. They help to break down debris on the forest floor. Look around to find these common and helpful organisms.

Fungi

"Fungi" is the plural form of the word fungus. Mushrooms are the most common forest fungi. There are about 14,000 known types! Mushrooms are actually the fruit of underground organisms. They make chemicals that break down fallen leaves and other debris.

Mold is another type of fungus. Mold grows in a fuzzy layer on rotting material. It is a sure sign of decay.

Lichen

Lichen is a mixture of fungus and algae. It often grows in crusty mats, but it can also be stringy or slimy. Lichen comes in many different colors.

LOOK AND COUNT

How many types of mushrooms can you find? How many lichens?

ACTIVITY:

Spore Prints

Mushrooms shed thousands of tiny seeds called spores from their undersides. The spores fall in patterns that match the mushroom's shape. Scientists capture these spore prints to identify the mushrooms they find in the wild.

Here's how to make your own spore prints using just a few simple materials.

CAUTION! Some wild mushrooms are poisonous, so check with an adult before doing this activity. You can also do this activity with a mushroom from a grocery store.

YOU WILL NEED
....
- Fresh mushroom, the type with gills
- Sheet of white paper
- Water
- Cup that is larger than the mushroom's cap
- Hairspray

How to do it

1 With a grown-up's help, cut the stem off the mushroom. Be very careful not to damage the fragile gills.

2 Lay a sheet of white paper on a flat surface where it will not be disturbed. Set the mushroom cap, gills down, on the paper.

3 Put a few drops of water on top of the mushroom. This will help it to open up and release its spores.

4 Cover the mushroom cap with a cup. This will stop air from blowing across the mushroom cap.

5 Let the mushroom cap sit undisturbed for 24 hours. Then lift the cup and the cap. Look at the paper. You should see a colorful spore print in the shape of the mushroom's gills.

6 Spray the spore print with hairspray to preserve it. Turn it into a greeting card or anything else you like.

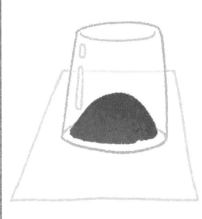

The Forest at Night

When night falls, many animals go to sleep, but others are just waking up and a whole new crew takes over. With a grown-up, take a night walk through the woods. What might you see and hear on your dark journey?

Owls

Hoot, hoot! Owls are on the prowl. Owls are nighttime birds that fly silently on thickly feathered wings. Shine a flashlight up into the tree canopy. Can you spot shining eyes peering down at you?

Wood Mice

Wood mice are small and quiet. They stick to heavy cover, where they will be safer from nighttime predators. These habits make them very difficult to spot. Find a still place and sit silently. Watch and wait—maybe you'll get lucky.

Foxes

Some foxes emerge from their dens at dusk and roam all night long, searching for food. Many foxes prowl in urban areas as well—when nighttime comes, you might be able to see a fox slinking down the street.

Bats

Bats are small, winged mammals that take to the air at night. You'll find them at the edges of the forest, where there is plenty of space to swoop and circle. If you are very still and very quiet, you may hear them squeaking. They use their squeaks like radar to help them find food.

Moths

Moths flitter and flutter through the forest trees. Unlike butterflies, moths are active at night. Moths have plump bodies—sometimes bats like to eat them as a snack!

Wild Boar

Wild boar are native to Europe, Asia, and parts of the United States and Australia. They are not quiet. They tromp through bushes with a loud crashing, bashing, and cracking. These big, wild pigs can be grouchy, so keep your distance if you hear a boar—or any large animal—approaching in the night.

Notes for Parents and Teachers

Here are some ideas to help you encourage a love of nature in children.

- ADVENTURE: Going out to explore should be an adventure that is in line with the developmental stage of the child. An adventure for a baby is lying on a blanket underneath trees. For a toddler it is taking a ramble through a park with plenty of time to pick up sticks and investigate. An adventure for a four-year-old might mean climbing the same tree for an hour. Don't wear yourself out planning a grand adventure when something simple will do!

- LET GO: Practice letting go. Given space to do so, kids will take the lead and delight in exploring. Research shows that kids who are free to take risks in their play (such as balancing on stepping stones across a creek) develop responsibility and judgment.

- SLOW DOWN: Abandon the idea of getting to a certain destination. The journey, and the time to explore, are what matter most in cultivating a deep connection to the natural world. When we hustle kids to hike to a given destination in a timely manner, our goals may run counter to young people's natural desire to investigate and sour them on spending time in nature.

- BUILD A ROUTINE: Look for ways to make nature a part of your daily or weekly routine. If nature-based learning is not a part of your school offerings, consider making time before or after school and on weekends. You can do this informally by taking a detour through a park or bird watching on your way to school, or formally by enrolling in an after-school program or starting a family nature club.

- RAIN OR SHINE: An old adage says, "There's no such thing as bad weather, just bad clothing." So, adjust your attitude, layer up, and enjoy exploring no matter the weather.

- MAKE TIME FOR NATURE: It's possible to find aspects of the natural world even in the midst of a packed schedule. Try leaving the house ten minutes early in the morning to look at the changing leaves and hunt for nuts and seeds. When planning social gatherings, choose an outdoor setting like a park. Park your car or get off transit a few blocks before your destination and enjoy the walk.

- EXPAND YOUR DEFINITION: Embrace the concept of "nearby nature" by noticing living creatures and seasonal changes in your backyard, a nearby park, or on your street.

- FIND COMMUNITY: Research forest schools and outdoor programs in your area—these are great places to meet new people and discover local nature areas.

- KEEP A JOURNAL: Start keeping a nature journal where you record your observations. Kids can carry blank journals and colored pencils, too. A journal should be the child's own book to use in any way they see fit, for things such as making notes, drawing, or adding photos.

- SIT STILL: Try introducing "sit spots" as an activity. Each person finds their own spot to settle down quietly for a set amount of time (five minutes is a good place to start). Prompt observation by asking children to tune into their senses, such as the feeling of breeze on their face or the wind in their hair.

Anna Sharratt
Founder of Free Forest School

Equipment

You don't need expensive equipment to learn about nature—it's about getting outside, exploring, and experimenting. While you might choose to bring some basic tools, leave toys and valuable possessions at home. This inspires creative play with found objects in nature. Here are suggestions for simple tools that might come in handy:

TOOLS

- Pens
- Pencils
- Paper
- Camera
- Magnifying glass
- Binoculars
- Flashlight
- Twine or cord
- Empty plastic containers from the recycling bin, such as 1-quart yogurt tubs
- Scissors
- Pocket knife
- Simple first-aid kit

CLOTHING AND EQUIPMENT

- Backpack
- Water bottle
- Waterproof jacket
- Waterproof footwear
- Long-sleeved top
- Long trousers
- Sweater
- Hat, gloves, and scarf for cold weather
- Hat and sunscreen for warm weather

Further information

For further information about forest schools and options in your local area, these programs are a great place to start:

Free Forest School
www.freeforestschool.org
Letting kids be kids, outdoors. Free Forest School ignites children's innate capacity to learn through unstructured play in nature, fostering healthy development and nurturing the next generation of creative thinkers, collaborative leaders, and environmental stewards.

Forest Schools Kindergarten
www.forestschoolskindergarten.com
Forest Schools Kindergarten gives children the time, space, and freedom to play while immersed in a natural environment.

Forest Schools Education
www.forestschools.com
A Forest School training provider with over 15 years of helping educators change the lives of those around them.

Index